Don't Ever Let Go

Don't Ever Let Go

Finding Freedom in Christ
Amidst the Trials of
Postpartum Depression

SHIRLEY MOTORCA

Charleston, SC
www.PalmettoPublishing.com

Don't Ever Let Go
Copyright © 2023 by Shirley Motorca

All rights reserved
No portion of this book may be reproduced, stored in a retrieval system, or transmitted in any form by any means–electronic, mechanical, photocopy, recording, or other–except for brief quotations in printed reviews, without prior permission of the author.

First Edition

Paperback ISBN: 979-8-8229-2004-0
eBook ISBN: 979-8-8229-2257-0

Table of Contents

Introduction   i

Part I – Search for Significance   1
Chapter 1 – He Cares for You   3
Chapter 2 – Who Turned Out the Lights?   19

Part II – True Love   35
Chapter 3 – The Father's Love   37
Chapter 4 – Total Surrender   47

Part III – Freedom in Christ   55
Chapter 5 – The Truth Will Set You Free   57
Chapter 6 – Renewing the Mind for a New Beginning   67

Introduction

Regardless of the scale, every individual will inevitably encounter and triumph over a challenging situation during their lifetime. And when we do, we become a living testimony, shining brighter with each step that we take. Sharing your testimony can provide hope, encouragement, strength, and power to someone facing their own trials and tribulations. For all who read this book, I pray it provides you with hope, healing, and a hunger and thirst for God, a commitment to pursue Him like never before. You serve a unique purpose and hold immense value. God knew you would be reading this book. To God be the glory.

PART I
Search for Significance

CHAPTER 1
He Cares for You

> *For God so [greatly] loved and dearly prized the world, that He [even] gave His [One and] only begotten Son, so that whoever believes and trusts in Him [as Savior] shall not perish, but have eternal life.*
>
> —John 3:16 (Amplified Bible)

Despite the abundance of information that is at our disposal, many unanswered questions remain. What am I here for? Who am I? Have you ever pondered something comparable, and if so, did you ever receive answers to those questions? If you, too, are seeking answers, I have good news for you. Those are questions that I, like many others, have pondered. In a subsequent chapter, I'll explain how those questions were answered as well as who provided the responses.

For the better part of my life, I've been preoccupied with the pursuit of resolving countless questions concerning the significance of existence and the role that I play in it. As a teenager I recall strolling along the sandy shores reflecting on the mysteries of life. I longed for my life to have meaning, and I wanted to know why I was here. Lost in a sea of uncertainty, I sought significance from all the wrong sources. This was a mistake.

I was born in Indonesia, a country that is well-known for both the natural beauty of its beaches and the intensity of its volcanoes. Sadly, I don't remember much from the years I spent living there. I was just four years old when I made the trip across the ocean to the United States with my parents, older brother, and sister. Having no idea where we were going or why, I, just like any other innocent child, placed my trust in my parents. Together we ventured towards Daytona Beach, Florida, where we set out to live the American Dream, as we had come to understand it.

My parents eventually had two more children, making me the middle child. Life takes on a whole new dynamic when you're no longer the youngest one in the family. When I was in elementary school, my family and I made the move to Ormond-by-the-Sea, a nearby city that is both lovely and quiet. I have so many fond memories of playing with my siblings, relatives, and friends there as a child. We used to spend hours playing at the beach, which was within walking distance of our home. Our home was where family would gather on holidays. My aunts, uncles, and cousins were always over. My mom would babysit my cousins, and we all enjoyed just being kids. Our regular sleepovers were something I looked forward to.

It wasn't until I was in the fourth grade that things began to gradually shift. You have to understand that we have an adversary known as the devil, and he enjoys secretly invading our territory in the hopes that no one will discover his presence.

> *The thief does not come except to steal, and to kill, and to destroy. I have come that they may have life, and that they may have it more abundantly.*
> —John 10:10 (New King James Version)

To gain entrance into a person's life, the devil needs nothing more than an opening in the door. The devil moves in slowly and makes his home in the mind and establishes a foothold there. The mind is a place where the devil can inflict damage on a person without that person even being aware of it happening. It's the little things that people think, say, or do when no one is watching that take them down the wrong path. One must be rooted in the Word and know their identity in Christ in order to make it in this world. Ideas and images from all across the world are continually being pushed on the general public. Pick up any magazine or get onto any social media platform to discover what the rest of the world considers to be *beautiful*. It's no surprise that so many people are suffering in silence.

I grew up in a home that was anything but normal. My father had a drinking problem and found it challenging to maintain employment. In addition to drinking, he also gambled regularly. With no family in the States to help her, my mother did the best she could to raise us and keep our family together. Growing up in a house full of children, I never felt loved. My parents never had deep conversations with me. I never felt secure enough to talk with my parents about what was in my heart. By the time we got around to talking, it was too late. I was in trouble by then. It is up to the parents to love, instruct, and guide their children to a relationship with Jesus Christ.

> *Train up a child in the way he should go: and when he is old, he will not depart from it.*
>
> —Proverbs 22:6 (NKJV)

As a young girl, I remember being so unhappy with my appearance. I considered myself to be unattractive and overweight, and I disliked the way my face was shaped. My face has always been more round, and it bothered me as a child.

I dreamed about looking like the people on the magazine covers who were tall and skinny. What started in elementary school followed me to middle school, high school, and college all the way up until I got married. I made the mistake of surrounding myself with the wrong kind of people, which led to my involvement in dangerous behaviors, such as drug use and partying, as well as relationships that were emotionally and physically abusive. I longed to be loved, so I searched for it in unhealthy relationships that ultimately resulted in utter disappointment.

By the age of eighteen, I wanted my life to end. I was put on antidepressants and was informed that I would need to be on them permanently. I later got off the medication, but those underlying issues were never dealt with. Still lost, not knowing what to do with my life, I decided to go to college. During the day, I led what the vast majority of people would consider to be a *normal* life. The nightlife was when my life felt like it was spinning out of control.

I had gotten myself involved in a relationship that was leading me deeper into a life I could never have imagined living. My nightlife consisted of working in some of the darkest nightclubs, where I would drink and do drugs. It was a dangerous lifestyle I was living behind closed doors. There were instances when I awoke in my room, but I had no memory of how I had gotten there. On many occasions, God chose to spare my life, and the specifics of some of those occurrences won't become clear to me until after I have arrived in heaven.

During a routine doctor's appointment, I discovered I was seven weeks pregnant. I was unsure of what to think or do. Confused and in disbelief, I made my way to an abortion clinic, and they confirmed I was seven weeks pregnant. The physician drastically decreased the ultrasound volume, so I was unable to hear the heartbeat. When I asked to see the ultrasound, the doctor refused. Despite the multitude of emotions I experienced, and my intuition urging me against it, I made the difficult decision to have an abortion. I walked out of that office that day feeling a heavy weight of shame and guilt about the choice I made. Looking back, I can see that it was a tremendous mistake that required me to do some serious soul-searching and inner healing.

The mother, when deciding to have an abortion, has the ability to make a choice. However, the precious life that is now developing within her does not have that same opportunity. No one is born by accident, regardless of what anyone says. God determines the exact time and place of each person's birth. The Lord is the one who created you and shaped you while you were still in your mother's womb (Psalm 139:13). There are alternative options and resources that can be utilized. I wish I'd known then what I know now. Assistance is available. If you have had an abortion, ask God to forgive you and forgive yourself. Don't be so hard on yourself. Instead, receive God's forgiveness and open your heart to His healing touch. I'll share with you how God healed me from the emotional scars left by that abortion later on.

They say it only takes one bad apple to spoil the whole bunch. Indeed, it is true that bad associations can have a detrimental effect on one's well-being. Having said that, it is necessary to understand that the decision to remain in toxic relationships is ultimately one that we make for ourselves.

> *Do not be deceived: "Bad company corrupts good morals."*
> —1 Corinthians 15:33
> (New American Standard Bible)

It is necessary for each of us to acknowledge that we are responsible for our own choices. Many people, including myself, continue to be in relationships despite the fact that they are not good for either party. Always keep in mind how valuable you are and take comfort in the knowledge that God wants nothing but the best for you. You shouldn't get involved with someone who treats you worse than you deserve to be treated. I made the decision to stay in an unhealthy relationship for much longer than I should have, one in which constant fighting and drinking were regular occurrences. At one point an argument led to the cops being called, and I was then arrested. That was enough for me. I knew I had to move on with my life, so I decided to enroll in court reporting school in Jacksonville,

Florida. That breakup left me feeling wounded and unmotivated to pursue new relationships. The pain of all the past mistakes I had made was repressed as I continued to go about my life.

Even the most traumatic circumstances can be transformed by God into opportunities for spiritual maturation and advancement.

> *And we know [with great confidence] that God [who is deeply concerned about us] causes all things to work together [as a plan] for good for those who love God, to those who are called according to His plan and purpose.*
> —Romans 8:28 (AMP)

I had become so accustomed to being hurt and mistreated that when God brought me the man who would be my future husband, I unintentionally blew him off. I was working as a leasing coordinator at an apartment community when I first started court reporting school. It was a normal, hot and sunny Sunday afternoon when a man who was hosting his nephews' birthday party came into the lobby and approached me. After using the helium machine on the property to fill the kids' balloons, he asked if I wanted to attend the birthday party. No way, I thought to myself. I had recently left an unhealthy relationship, and I honestly did not want to get involved in another relationship. I made an excuse and didn't think twice about it. After handing me his business card, I continued on with my day.

Four months passed before this man, whom I had brushed aside, came to my mind. Having found an excuse to call him to alter some clothes, I called the number that was on the business card he gave me months prior. To my surprise, he answered the phone, and I introduced myself. He stated that he recognized me from the tone of my voice. We finally had the chance to meet up for dinner. Shortly thereafter, we began dating.

After two months of dating, I asked him to take me to church. He drove me to a local church. I had no idea that that day would be a day that would change the course of my life. I sat through the service, and at the end of the service, they did an altar call. I felt the Lord's call in my heart. As I sat in my chair, I became aware of how rapidly my heart was beating. I had no idea what was happening. I stood up and made my way to the front, crying and trembling on the inside. Anyone who knows me knows that I am not inclined to do such a thing. In college, I had to take speech class twice in order to pass. That's how terrified I was to speak in public. That day the Holy Spirit tugged on my heart, and I said yes to Him. I received Jesus as my Lord and Savior on June 12, 2005, and I'll never forget that day. You see, God has a plan for you, and it's good. If you haven't received Jesus into your life, it's never too late. Simply ask Him to forgive you of all your sins and to come into your heart so that He can be Lord of your life.

> *"For I know the plans and thoughts that I have for you," says the Lord, "plans for peace and well-being and not for disaster, to give you a future and a hope."*
> —Jeremiah 29:11 (AMP)

That same year, Daniel proposed to me and I, of course, said yes. I do not advise anyone to go through what we did and stay engaged for seven years. I also believe that a couple should wait until they are married before moving in together. On August 12, 2012, we exchanged vows in the presence of God and all of our guests. That was one of the happiest days of my life.

When two people join together in marriage and become one, all the relationship issues do not simply vanish. We must address our issues or else they follow us into our marriage. I had so many problems and carried all of my baggage into our marriage. For years, we fought more than I'd like to admit. I insisted on being right all the time, and it was always my way or the highway. We all know that doesn't work well in any relationship, let alone a marriage. As a result, I was completely at a loss as to how to handle my emotions. My emotions would fluctuate wildly from calm one moment to boiling anger the next. My thoughts and actions were completely out of control. I would lose my temper and storm out of the house. I would declare I was leaving and would never return. I always came back though. The words I spoke were insensitive and destructive. We have to stop thinking of ourselves and think about others, think about how they feel when we say or do the things we do.

The torments I had struggled with were starting to resurface. It was common for me to go to bed and wake up unable to move. I remember waking up from nightmares screaming Jesus's name. There is power in the name of Jesus, and saying *Jesus* would free me and allow me to awaken. In the past, I had opened up the door to the enemy by allowing tarot card readings, by seeing a hypnotist on many occasions, and by trying crystal healing techniques. The Bible is very clear about this.

In Leviticus 19:31 (AMP), it says, "Do not turn to mediums [who pretend to consult the dead] or to spiritists [who have spirits of divination]; do not seek them out to be defiled by them. I am the Lord your God."

This is a serious matter, and so many people, even Christians, are entertaining such practices, believing it's okay when it's actually very dangerous. Please stop, read the prayer at the end of this chapter, and turn from wickedness before it's too late.

My husband was, and continues to be, extremely patient with me. After everything I had put him through, I questioned his decision to stay with me. What he said next completely floored me. According to Daniel, God told him to be patient with me. How incredibly patient he has been with me. I give God the glory for uniting my husband and me.

Not long after my marriage, my mom was diagnosed with stage 4 lung cancer. The news was devastating. My mom's health problems had begun long before I got married. She suffered from a persistent cough. Never in a million years did I imagine that this would happen to my mom. As I matured and realized how fortunate I was to have her as my mother, my relationship with her grew.

As it was in her best interest, my mom moved in with my older sister, who is a nurse, to start receiving cancer treatments. I tried to visit my mom as often as I could while she underwent treatment. The holidays with my family were never the same once my mother began chemotherapy and radiation treatments. It hurt to witness my mother deteriorate before my eyes. She had lost so much weight, and her hair was falling out. I felt so helpless.

My mother sat and stared at the food on her plate while everyone else was enjoying their Thanksgiving dinner. Sweets and fried food were my mom's downfall, but she no longer had a desire for them. She stated that everything tasted bitter. Despite her strength, my mother was not treated with the respect she deserved. Bitterness is defined as anger and disappointment at being treated unfairly; resentment. If you are treated unfairly, do not allow bitterness to set in. Instead, repent, give it to God, and move on.

In the beginning of 2013, I found out I was pregnant with our first child. I was so excited to share the news with my mom. I wanted her to meet my son. All I could think about was whether she was going to live long enough to meet him.

While my mother was undergoing cancer treatment, I made frequent trips to Ormond Beach to be at her side. My sisters and I would take turns driving her to her chemotherapy and radiation treatments. There were many sleepless nights, either crying in a hospital room or at my sister's house, where my mom was eventually placed in hospice care. Not long after she was placed in hospice care, my mom was hospitalized due to pneumonia. The doctors didn't think she was going to make it, but she did. She was a fighter. That year went by so fast. The pregnancy sometimes slipped my mind. Thinking of my mom was all I could do. She would call and leave me voice messages, making sure I made it home safely. Oh, the sweet sound of her voice. I can still hear it softly calling out my name.

It was painful at times to watch my mom transition. I knew she was going to be spending eternity with Jesus, and that gave me peace. But when she would speak in her native language of Indonesia, which I was not familiar with, and make the end-of-life gurgling noise, it was disheartening. No one wants to witness that, especially when it is their loved one. When her life was coming to an end, I stayed by her side. It was a typical morning at my sister's house. My sister left the house to take her eldest son to school. I had just gotten up, and as soon as I stepped out of the room, my mom took her last breath. I could not believe it. I grabbed the pulse oximeter and slipped it on her finger. The reading showed she had no pulse. I called my older sister, but she didn't answer. When she returned home, I informed her that I was trying to call her to give her the news. It was right before Christmas in 2013, and I had so much guilt as well as a lot of questions that needed to be answered. How could this happen? Why did my mother wait until there was no one else in the room before she took her final breath?

My mom was a beautiful woman, both inside and out. It grieved me terribly to watch her go through treatments and to see her lose a significant amount of weight, her thick black hair, her strength, and her confidence. She was only given one more year after she started the cancer treatments. I don't know what was worse, the cancer itself or watching what the treatments did to her body. It hurt to watch her suffer. After a yearlong battle with lung cancer, my mom passed away on December 12, 2013. I was nearing the end of my pregnancy, and my siblings and I had to make funeral arrangements. That year my family and I celebrated Christmas without our mother for the first time. It was different from what I had expected. It was clear that my mother's life had not been lived to its full potential. She was still so young. She died at the age of fifty-seven.

As 2013 came to a close, I received the news that my son was in a breech position, so I did what any mother would do to try to get their baby to turn. I frequently went to a chiropractor and tried a variety of exercises on a regular basis in the hopes that it would help him turn position. Four days before my son's due date, I started to feel really uncomfortable and was starting to feel a lot of pressure. The contractions started in the early morning hours. Not wanting to wake up my husband or bother calling my doula, I tossed and turned on the sofa until the sun came up. Not knowing whether I was in labor or not, I called my OB-GYN's office and was advised to come in to the office for an examination. Upon my arrival, I was informed that I was already four centimeters dilated and needed to be taken to the hospital since my baby was in a breech position.

At that moment, my heart sank. How could this be? I was still grieving the loss of my mother. I wasn't prepared to have a baby quite yet and had not planned for a C-section. I had a birth plan, and nothing on it referenced a C-section. That day my son was delivered via a C-section, and all I could do was cry. No matter how hard I tried, I just couldn't stop thinking about how much I missed my mom. Why couldn't she have lived a month longer so she could have met my son?

Fear gripped me, and I felt helpless. I had convinced myself that I was ready to become a mother, but the truth was quite different. In spite of my extensive reading, I had never even changed a baby's diaper. Nothing could have prepared me for what was about to unfold. The first several days in the hospital were quite challenging. My son was crying nonstop, and I had no idea what to do. I asked the nurse if there was something wrong because he was crying so much, and she responded that that's what newborns do. The first night in the hospital room, I cried myself to sleep. My heart ached for my mom. The loss of her left a void in my life. Breastfeeding was proving to be a real challenge for me. I wanted to call my mother and ask for guidance, but I couldn't. When something is taken away from us, only then do we realize how valuable it is.

Prayer:

Heavenly Father, thank You for loving me more than anyone ever could. If I have in any way, whether intentionally or unintentionally, helped the enemy by opening any door, please forgive me. In the name of Jesus Christ, I reject whatever relationship I may have had with witchcraft and I shut the doors that were formerly open to the devil. Show me what it means to be loved by You and fill every void in my heart with Your love. Teach me what it means to be loved by You. Help me to appreciate each day that You have given me and to make the most of the time I have here on earth. In Jesus's name. Amen.

CHAPTER 2
Who Turned Out the Lights?

> *This is the message [of God's promised revelation] which we have heard from Him and now announce to you, that God is Light [He is holy, His message is truthful, He is perfect in righteousness], and in Him there is no darkness at all [no sin, no wickedness, no imperfection].*
> —1 John 1:5 (AMP)

Before I knew it, my husband and I were on our way home from the hospital with our son. Life would never be the same. I returned home with a newborn who rarely napped. He developed torticollis, which resulted in his head tilting to the right. I took him to the chiropractor on a regular basis to have him adjusted in order to correct the problem.

Even with the assistance of the hospital's lactation consultant, my doula, a La Leche League representative, our pediatrician, and my son's lip- and tongue-tie, which was supposed to help him nurse properly, he still wouldn't latch on without experiencing pain. I felt defeated. Although the pain was intense, I continued breastfeeding. My nipples were missing chunks and occasionally bled. All that came to an end when my son turned five months old, and I started giving him formula. If necessary, there is no shame in feeding a newborn formula. I fed it to him until he turned one, and he's healthy. In their efforts to do the *right* thing, mothers often impose unnecessary stress on themselves. When it comes down to it, who decides what is best for your child? Do what is best for you and your family and don't feel guilty about your decision.

It seemed that just when I managed to resolve one problem, another would arise. I thought I was losing my mind from hearing my son cry all day. He was a colicky baby. The crying would begin around six in the evening and last for what seemed like eternity. When my husband got home from work, I'd hand our son to him. Though I tried to mask my distress, I desperately needed assistance. Exhaustion began to set in, and I quickly felt my identity was slipping away.

Everyone kept telling me it was just the *baby blues*, so I assumed I'd soon feel like myself again. I anticipated taking maternity leave and then returning to work as a court reporter after a few months. That did not come to pass. I went against everything I ever claimed I would never do and became a stay-at-home mom. My experience has taught me that it is best to avoid using the word *never*.

I felt a sense of inadequacy in my role as a mother. I was beginning to feel like I was drowning in a sea of problems. Once I decided to quit breastfeeding, things quickly went downhill. I tried to slowly wean my son, but that didn't happen. Stopping abruptly only put more fuel on the fire, and what I thought was normal turned into a deeper level of depression. Once again, I felt like a failure.

The negative voices I kept hearing became increasingly louder. I couldn't shut it off. For most of my life, I tried to ignore the dark and destructive thoughts that often tormented my mind. This time though, all I kept hearing were the following: I am not a good mother. I am a failure. I am not good enough. My family would be better off without me. Despite the fact that they were all lies, I continued to believe them.

We must be cautious of social media's deceptive effects. I would log on and begin comparing myself against other moms who appeared to have it all together. After giving birth, society expects new mothers to conform to particular standards of behavior and appearance. You and I both know that no one ever posts the harsh reality of motherhood. All I ever came across were posts about women talking about how happy they were to become mothers. As for me, I was counting down the hours until the day was over. The truth of how challenging motherhood can be is not discussed openly enough.

Aside from when my husband returned home from work, I had no adult interaction. We were not created to be alone and isolated. We need healthy relationships, fellowship with like-minded people and others to sharpen us.

> *You use steel to sharpen steel, and one friend sharpens another.*
> —Proverbs 27:17 (The Message)

Isolation kept me confined to the four walls of our home, which seemed to get increasingly smaller and difficult to breathe in. Completely overwhelmed, all I wanted to do was sleep the day away.

Months went by, and instead of feeling enjoyment or a little more at ease, worry, fear, and anxiety started to take over. The days seemed so long. Minutes felt like hours, hours like days, and days like months. Every time I looked at the clock, I found myself wishing it was much later. I kept looking forward to the next holiday, hoping it would get easier as we approached the one-year mark. Then a holiday would arrive, and I'd still be miserable. For some reason, I assumed that once my son turned one, everything would return to normal.

Going from working and being busy all day to staying at home and caring for an infant 24-7 had completely changed my life. Before having a child, I was busy but in a different way. My mind finally had a chance to slow down, but all the thoughts that were going through my head were troubling me.

When you are always busy and on the move, you never really have the time to sit and think about things. That is dangerous. We need time to slow down and simply be still.

> *Be still and know (recognize, understand) that I am God. I will be exalted among the nations! I will be exalted in the earth.*
> —Psalm 46:10 (AMP)

It was evident that my days were getting darker, as I slid into a pit that no one knew about. I didn't want to show how miserable I felt. I was too concerned about other people's opinions of me. The only times I really left the house were to take my son to the chiropractor and the pediatrician. When I did venture out, it was never for very long.

A simple trip to the grocery store brought on anxiety. It was much less stressful to call my husband and ask that he pick up groceries. He would come home from a long day and either prepare a meal or order takeout. The activities that used to bring me joy no longer did. I lost sense of what was going on around me and felt numb. I was so ashamed and afraid of what I was experiencing, so I kept my feelings and actions hidden from everyone, including my husband. Although my actions were abnormal, I was in such denial. I just assumed that everything would eventually return to normal.

My husband was completely unaware of all of the dangerous things I was doing. I would tell him that I needed time to be by myself, and I would leave the house. I wasted hours aimlessly driving, thinking about the possibility of ending my own life. As I passed by several highway ramps and trees, I wondered if I would die if I drove off the ramp or into a tree. To find suicide methods, I looked them up on the internet. I'd rummage through our medicine cabinet to see if there was anything I could mix and ingest to put an end to the pain I was experiencing. My husband was beginning to notice that what I was going through was much more severe than the baby blues.

The voices in my head were overpowering and followed me everywhere I went. I could not escape the agony. So many battles occur in the mind. We must learn to recognize where the voices are coming from. In the absence of acknowledgment, the voices grow in volume until you eventually give in to them.

I was convinced that the only thing I was any good at was crying, and I had reached the point where I no longer wanted to be a mother. I longed for the days when my life was more like it had been in the past. I was completely lost and didn't even recognize myself. I was now referred to as a mother, despite the fact that I was not particularly successful at my new role.

Before experiencing my own panic attack, I had no idea what they were like. I avoided leaving the house because I didn't want to experience another episode, and I believed that being at home with my son would be the safest place for us. There were moments when I felt like I couldn't catch my breath, and the world around me didn't appear quite right. My vision for life was starting to diminish. Everyday tasks were becoming increasingly difficult for me to do.

I started to worry excessively over minor issues. Throughout the day, I would frequently phone my loved ones and ask them the same set of questions. I wanted to make sure that everything I did was in line with what I had read in books and on the internet, which I now know is a recipe for disaster because every child is different and so is everyone's living situation.

I truly believed my family would be better off without me. I was desperately trying to mask my emotions. I did what the majority of women do: showered, got dressed, applied makeup, and went to my scheduled appointments. I was leading a double life, concealing the real me behind a carefully painted mask. I was living an illusion. It's true that a person's makeup can hide their true character, but mine wasn't fooling anyone anymore. Eventually, my son's chiropractor, pediatrician, and my husband began to suspect something was wrong with me.

There is a purpose behind why God places certain people in our lives. Our chiropractor shared a personal story with me and offered words of encouragement and reassurance that everything was going to be okay. During each of my son's checkups, his pediatrician would ask about how I was doing and spend a significant amount of time talking with me. When we give someone our full attention and listen to what they have to say, we learn more about them and are better able to help them.

I was tired of pretending like I was okay when deep down, I was in turmoil. I was afraid of being judged as a bad mother if I admitted how I really felt, so I kept my feelings bottled inside. My whole life up to that point had been influenced by the buildup of pain, and I often found myself experiencing a range of mixed emotions. I did my best to bury years' worth of poor choices, heartache, and trauma, but they were all beginning to resurface. Never in a million years did I consider harming my child. I simply could no longer bear to dwell in the depths of despair. I realized the severity of the situation and that I could no longer hide it from everyone.

Being mentally tormented in seclusion was unbearable, especially with an infant, so I finally decided to get help. My initial visit was to a Christian counselor. I always felt great after a session with her. When I returned home, the mental anguish would resume, and I would call upon her once more. She acknowledged that I was dealing with a situation that was outside of her area of expertise and suggested that I seek counsel from other sources.

I would sit and allow my mind to wander, which is exactly what the enemy wanted. My mind was inundated with a multitude of toxic thoughts. I'd be fine one second, and then the next I'd realize I needed to get up and move around in order to pull my attention away from whatever was going through my head. It seemed like I was going crazy.

I chose to attend a local mom's support group. That's where I connected with a lady who was willing to listen to what I was going through. We also met at a coffee shop, where we sat and chatted for quite some time. She urged me to seek professional assistance.

After leaving the coffee shop, I headed straight for the emergency room. As I pulled into the hospital's parking garage and made my way inside the main building, my mind starting racing. There was a tug-of-war going on in my mind. I took a seat, filled out the registration form, and waited for my name to be called. After calling my name, the nurse started collecting my vital signs and questioning me about my condition. In addition, she was interested in hearing about my experiences with postpartum depression. Since I would rather not have been there, I lied and said I had no problems whatsoever when asked about it. I came to the conclusion that if I went in, they would see me and release me. In such a scenario, I would be in a position to claim that I had been seen, that everything was well, and I was free to return home.

My worst fear was that I would be taken to a mental institution and separated from my baby. The second nurse

I met that night in the hospital told me about her personal experience with a mother who had committed suicide. She went on to say that she was concerned for my safety and the safety of others. She remained with me after hours in the emergency room until my husband arrived there. I had never met this nurse before, yet she wanted to make sure I received the help I so desperately needed.

After speaking with the head of the maternity unit and reassuring her that I did not pose any kind of threat to anyone, I was permitted to leave the hospital. I felt a sense of relief. A large portion of that year was a blur.

My husband encouraged me to be honest about how I was feeling. I had no idea what was going to happen to me, so I talked my way out of it, and I was discharged because I *looked* as though I was fine. I hated to do it, but I was afraid they'd take my child otherwise.

My husband and I headed back home, but we both knew I needed to get assistance from someone qualified to treat postpartum depression. He called someone he knew, and she connected us with a psychologist and a psychiatrist. After much resistance on my part, I ultimately gave in and agreed to meet with them for a more in-depth assessment. I was willing to try anything in the hopes of regaining my life. This husband-and-wife combination operated their own practice and collaborated in its operation. My husband scheduled the appointment for me, and the two of us went there together. After discussing my options with both the psychologist and psychiatrist, we decided that outpatient services, where I could remain at home with my family, would be more beneficial than inpatient care. This pair remarked that my spouse must be an extremely strong man in order to carry out what he was doing. He was determined to help me get the support I needed.

I continued to attend my weekly counseling sessions, as they tested various antidepressants on me. When one medication did not work, I had to try another one because the side effects were so bad. Nobody, including myself, wants to spend the entire day feeling nauseous and vomiting. I was responsible for taking care of a newborn, yet all I wanted to do was sleep and stay in bed. The negative effects of the antidepressants only served to heighten my thoughts of suicide.

Day-to-day activities were difficult for me to complete on my own. During the day, my elderly father-in-law would come over and entertain my son while I lay in bed miserable. Because I was having trouble taking care of both myself and my son, my husband would come home from work several times a day to help feed our son. Nothing could calm the mental chaos I was experiencing. I was advised that the prescribed antidepressant would be effective, but it would take some time before I saw any results. Meanwhile, I felt as though the world were caving in on me. It was becoming more and more obvious that I was starting to lose touch with reality.

God has blessed me with the sweetest child. He wanted nothing more than to laugh and play as well as to be loved and cared for. As my son reached one milestone after another, I became aware that he was beginning to comprehend more about the world around him. I was conscious of the fact that he deserved the very best version of me.

After participating in those counseling sessions for a considerable amount of time, I ultimately said, "Enough is enough. I cannot take it any longer." There is no shame in seeking alternative methods of healing in the natural world like I did. However, I came to understand that the battle was a spiritual one, and I realized that this was the approach I needed to take in order to win. According to *Merriam-Webster*, depression is a state of feeling sad. Depression can cause anger and anxiety and make a person feel hopeless, making it difficult to live a normal life. Depression is a tormenting spirit. If you're struggling with depression, arm yourself with the Word of God to defeat the spiritual warfare against the devil. The Bible has so much to say about depression.

> *Anxiety in a man's heart weighs it down, but a good (encouraging) word makes it glad.*
> —Proverbs 12:25 (AMP)

> *A heart full of joy and goodness makes a cheerful face, but when a heart is full of sadness the spirit is crushed.*
> —Proverbs 15:13 (AMP)

> *A happy heart is good medicine and a joyful mind causes healing, but a broken spirit dries up the bones.*
> —Proverbs 17:22 (AMP)

Only by putting my faith, confidence, and trust in God could I hope to make it through this incredibly difficult time in my life. I had exhausted all of my options, but none of them had been successful. My quest to find the most suitable antidepressant was unsuccessful, particularly given the fact that I have a high level of sensitivity to medication.

I have nothing against medical care or taking medication when necessary, and I would not advise you to stop taking the medication that are currently prescribed to you. If it is necessary, I will seek medical attention. In addition, I believe there are many different ways to receive healing. Medication and therapy could be the answer for one individual. What I call the *three F's*—my family, my friends, and, most importantly, my faith in Jesus—have been my source of healing. Because this is a group effort, it is important that the person who is suffering from postpartum depression, as well as the individuals who care about that person, have the opportunity to participate in the decision-making process. There is no reason to feel guilty about seeking help from a therapist or doctor. God will meet you wherever you are in your spiritual journey.

As for me, I was determined to live and break free from the shackles that had been placed around my heart and soul. I made the decision to discontinue the medications along with my appointments with the psychologist and the psychiatrist. I would not advise anyone to do that unless they felt led by the Holy Spirit and have support from their loved ones. I have been blessed with a strong husband who supported me and believed that God would stand by me no matter what. I had everything to gain and nothing to lose in this situation.

Both Daniel and I are fortunate to have good friends who are strong people of faith. A friend of Daniel's started sending me teachings from a well-known minister by the name of Andrew Wommack, who is widely known for teaching the full gospel. Despite the fact that it was fundamental teaching on healing, I had never come across it before that point. I made it a point to start nourishing my spirit with the truth.

The enemy desires for us to remain in darkness. We must not be deceived. Falsehoods are the work of the enemy. The Holy Spirit brings illumination and truth. He exposes all deception. Because God loves you, you can have hope. God's mercy and grace give you a reason to believe in a more promising future. Despite how obvious it may appear, we frequently fail to take this into account and instead look for someone—or even God—to place the blame on for the tragedies that take place in the world.

The Bible says:

> *My people are destroyed for lack of knowledge: because thou hast rejected knowledge, I will also reject thee, that thou shalt be no priest to me: seeing thou hast forgotten the law of thy God, I will also forget thy children.*
> —Hosea 4:6 (Authorized Version)

Prayer:

Father, open my eyes to the truth. Forgive me if I have ever held You or anybody else responsible for anything negative that has occurred in my life or the lives of those I care about. Bring to my attention all of the lies that I have believed and accepted so that I can replace them with the truth. In Jesus's name. Amen.

PART II
True Love

CHAPTER 3
The Father's Love

> *The Lord appeared to me (Israel) from ages past, saying,*
> *"I have loved you with an everlasting love;*
> *Therefore with lovingkindness*
> *I have drawn you and continued*
> *My faithfulness to you."*
>
> —Jeremiah 31:3 (AMP)

I set out to discover God. I was determined to make a change and find freedom from the oppression. I needed Him more than anything. I simply could not function in this world without Him. The longer I spent in His company, the deeper my affection for Him became. When my son would go down for a nap, I would use that time to go and just be with Jesus. I would spend the whole day listening to and watching different ministers on the television, nourishing my soul with the Word of God. During the time that I was listening to these ministers, I would take notes as they shared their wisdom. I yearned for a relationship with God.

I recall a particular day while my son was asleep, and I was sitting on a chair in our living room, absolutely drenched in tears, praying to God to take away the pain that I was experiencing. It was a desperate plea for help that I was making. I cried out to God and asked Him to intervene, saying, "God, if you're here, do something." What I didn't anticipate was for Him to put his arms around me. I was caught off guard. I had never experienced love like this before, and I couldn't get enough of it. As I sat there, I let myself soak in the love of the Father. Those twenty minutes made a long-lasting impression on me, one that I will never forget and one that I will never lose. I was hoping it wouldn't come to an end. I prayed, *God, don't ever let go!* After that, I became aware of the close proximity of His presence. After you have experienced the depth of His love for you, you will be in a position to help others receive the love He has for them.

Following that encounter, I began to make use of my faith in order to displace the lies and destructive beliefs I had about myself and my circumstances with the truth that is found in the Bible. I was attempting to deepen my understanding of the Word and soak everything in, but at the time, I did not have a solid foundation on which to build upon. It is not God's desire for us to just turn to Him in times of trouble. Unfortunately, I had been doing that for such a significant portion of my life up until that point.

I would spend time with Him on a daily basis. When God would make His presence known, I often found that I was unable to move. I would feel the heavy weight of God's presence. There is no language that can adequately express the glory of God, the beauty and splendor that He is. During those times, I felt an overwhelming sense of love, affection, and security. Those encounters left me with the impression that nothing else could possibly hold any more significance than spending time with Him.

These verses are a perfect summary of what I was experiencing, as I spent time with the One my soul yearned for:

> *I am standing in absolute stillness, silent before the one I love, waiting as long as it takes for him to rescue me. Only God is my Savior, and he will not fail me. For he alone is my safe place. His wrap-around presence always protects me as my champion defender. There's no risk of failure with God! So why would I let worry paralyze me, even when troubles multiply around me? God's glory is all around me! His wrap-around presence is all I need, for the Lord is my Savior, my hero, and my life-giving strength. Join me, everyone! Trust only in God every moment! Tell him all your troubles and*

> *pour out your heart-longings to him.*
> *Believe me when I tell you—he will help*
> *you!*
>
> —Psalm 62:5–8
> (The Passion Translation)

The importance of maintaining positive relationships cannot be overstated. There was a point in time when my father reported me missing to authorities. It wasn't until I got pulled over that I found out. I wasn't going over the posted speed limit. When the police officer approached my window, he stated that he ran my tag, and the database indicated I was missing. You see, if I had had a healthy relationship with my biological father, we would have been communicating, and he would have been aware of where I was. Not only was I rebellious toward him, but we also did not have any kind of relationship. Therefore, my father was never aware of my whereabouts.

Please know that our Heavenly Father desires a personal relationship with you. He wants you to come near to Him. Tell Him everything, both the good and the bad. To approach God, perfection is not a prerequisite. He is already well familiar with you, down to the smallest detail, such as the exact number of hairs on your head.

> *But [even] the very hairs of your head are all numbered. Do not be struck with fear or seized with alarm; you are of greater worth than many [flocks] of sparrows.*
> —Luke 12:7
> (Amplified Bible Classic Edition)

Do you feel you've been afflicted? You may be asking yourself, What does that even mean? *Merriam-Webster* defines *afflicted* as being grievously affected or troubled, as being mentally or physically impaired, and as people who are ill or suffering.

> *All the days of the afflicted are bad,*
> *but a glad heart has a continual feast*
> *[regardless of the circumstances].*
> —Proverbs 15:15 (AMP)

You can choose to have a joyful heart no matter what your circumstances are. I want to encourage you to start devoting some of your time spending it with Jesus. He loves you more than anybody else could ever love you. If you are hurting and feel unwanted or hopeless, draw near to God so He can heal your wounds and make you whole. He is the only one who can save you. Coming to Him at any point is never too late. You are very special to God, and He desires to have intimate fellowship with you.

I would consistently prioritize spending time with Him. As I quieted my mind, invited the Holy Spirit, and waited on Him, He came and shifted the atmosphere around me. There was no need to exchange words. Each time I met with Him, I could sense a deep inner healing taking place. Such peace would surround me. As I focused my attention on Jesus, I became increasingly aware of His presence within me. His breath became my own. It was almost as if I wasn't taking any breaths at all. As I stood in awe by the glory that He radiated, He was ministering to the most inward parts of my soul. The glory of the Lord is made known in His very presence as a revelation of His majesty. Jesus is the source of every good and perfect gift.

> *You will show me the path of life; In Your presence is fullness of joy;*
> *In Your right hand there are pleasures forevermore.*
> —Psalm 16:11 (AMP)

I encourage you to make an effort to find a quiet, peaceful place where you can spend time with Jesus. Close your eyes, turn your attention inward, and invite and allow the

Holy Spirit to fill you to overflowing. Just take a few deep breaths, focusing your attention on Jesus as you inhale and exhale slowly. Surrender your entire being to Him and allow Him to minister to you. He will take you to greater heights than you have ever seen or experienced before. Take your time and enjoy Him. Take in the glory of God's presence, and simply rest in the confidence that you are in His care. A good habit to get into is to pay attention to what you are seeing and listening to at all times. Play worship music throughout your home, and you will be able to sense a shift in the atmosphere around you.

Everything that had been missing in my relationship with my earthly father was graciously made available to me by our Heavenly Father. Jesus is the ultimate source of wisdom, yet so often we go to others for direction when what we really need is found in Him. Dealing with the underlying issues was not an easy task. After confessing my sins and turning my life over to Jesus, I was at last able to experience peace within myself. Finally, I was able to begin living again without being hindered by my past. Because of Jesus, all of our sins have been forgiven. The word *all* refers to everything, regardless of how large or tiny it may be. Knowing that anything and everything I had ever done wrong was forgiven gave me the greatest sense of freedom.

When you were dead in your sins and in the uncircumcision of your flesh

> *(worldliness, manner of life), God made you alive together with Christ, having [freely] forgiven us all our sins, having canceled out the certificate of debt consisting of legal demands [which were in force] against us and which were hostile to us. And this certificate He has set aside and completely removed by nailing it to the cross.*
> —Colossians 2:13–14 (AMP)

Jesus prepared the way for us to live free and remains steadfast in His commitment to forgive us. One layer at a time, shame and guilt were peeling away. The power of repentance is incredible. As time went on, I started noticing how much lighter my body felt. The burdens that I had carried on my shoulders from my past were gradually being lifted off.

I would not be here today to testify to the goodness of God if it were not for the grace He has shown me. Dear friend, know that God loves you. He knows what you have been through. He wants to comfort you and give you a new identity that is rooted in Him. Even if your life is a complete disaster, God is with you and has promised that He would never abandon you. His love for you is unconditional and does not require any actions on your part to earn it.

> *It is the Lord who goes before you; He will be with you. He will not fail you or abandon you. Do not fear or be dismayed.*
> —Deuteronomy 31:8 (AMP)

Prayer:

Holy Spirit, as I continue on my journey to seek truth, I humbly submit myself to Your direction so that I may arrive at my destination. Thank You for guiding me. Uncover the hidden mysteries that have been tucked within the Word. I desire to know You more intimately. Teach me how to hear and obey You. In Jesus's name. Amen.

CHAPTER 4
Total Surrender

> *Humble yourselves [with an attitude of repentance and insignificance] in the presence of the Lord, and He will exalt you [He will lift you up, He will give you purpose].*
>
> —James 4:10 (AMP)

Even when we are far from Him, God relentlessly pursues us. We love because He first loved us (1 John 4:19). God is after your heart. When you surrender and allow Him to work in and through you, He will. He will not force Himself on you, nor will He make you do anything against your own free will. I recall praying and asking God to heal me, and I sensed Him saying that my healing would come from within. It was as if someone had flicked on a light switch. My healing would originate from within me, from God who resides in me. He was already a part of me from the time I invited Jesus into my heart, and Jesus had already died so that I might be healed. When I was finally able to let go of trying to control my life and give God permission to work in it, that's when I noticed God's hand at work.

Even though I was hopping from one person to the next in search of help, no one could give me what it was that I was looking for. Since Jesus had already paid the price for everything I needed, there was no cost for me to receive it. My life began to take a new direction the moment I admitted to God that I couldn't do this on my own and began to put my trust in Him.

Even after being saved for a considerable amount of time, I continued to live in ignorance. Nevertheless, Jesus was there, ready to embrace and welcome me with open arms. You can expect the same treatment from Him. The Lord longs to be gracious to you. What God can accomplish in a split second is far more than anything we could accomplish in a lifetime. Through Jesus, healing is made available to all who will receive it.

Healing is a process, and just like any other process, it requires time to be completed. We are made up of our spirit, our soul, and our body. The condition of our soul—which is comprised of our mind, will, emotions, and imagination—has an impact on the degree to which we are able to heal from a physical or mental condition. The Holy Spirit plays an integral part throughout the process of healing, working within the lives of each individual. Once you have your salvation secured, the next step on the path to sanctification is obedience to God's will. Your existing situation may not change overnight, but when you put your faith and confidence in God first, everything else in your life will work out the way it's supposed to. Above all else, your primary call is to Jesus.

> *And Jesus replied to him, "You shall love the Lord your God with all your heart, and with all your soul, and with all your mind." This is the first and greatest commandment. The second is like it, "You shall love your neighbor as yourself [that is, unselfishly seek the best or higher good for others]." The whole Law and the [writings of the] Prophets depend on these two commandments.*
> —Matthew 22:37–40 (AMP)

As you obey, your priorities will shift. Don't be surprised if you find yourself spending less time with people than you used to. We will meet people throughout our lives that have the potential to either tear us down or lift us up. I had to discover that the hard way. When facing trials, it is crucial to surround yourself with uplifting influences rather than allowing yourself to be pulled further into despair. There will come a time when some people in your life will no longer be present. People enter our lives for different reasons, be it for a short time, a long time, or even forever. Yes, there is a season for everything.

> *To everything there is a season, and a time to every purpose under the heaven.*
> —Ecclesiastes 3:1 (AV)

It is essential to populate your inner circle with people who will propel you to greater heights. It is up to you to determine who should or should not be a part of your life at any particular point along your path, regardless of where you are in your journey. You can't expect everyone to agree with you or even understand where you're headed.

When you start devoting more of your time to pursuits that have an eternal impact, you'll find that you have less time for some of the things you used to enjoy doing. Every day, we are all allotted the same amount of time to spend as we see fit. It is entirely up to you to decide how you will spend the time that is available to you. Given that our world is full of so much noise and distraction, it is appropriate to be purposeful in the manner that we nurture our friendship with the Holy Spirit.

Everything in today's world moves at such a rapid pace, and everyone seems to be in such a rush. We need to take some deep breaths and reconnect ourselves with the One who will put us in our proper places. When our lives are so hectic, we don't give ourselves the chance to develop new habits or ways of thinking. As we spend more time with Jesus, we experience spiritual growth. He transforms us from the inside out, leading us from one level of glory to the next. As we progress spiritually, our aspirations begin to align more closely with those of God.

Living a peaceful, quiet life can be incredibly rewarding, as it allows you to escape the constant busyness and noise that often surrounds us in the world. Some individuals have a strong desire to be the focal point of attention and often strive to please others. Once you discover your identity in Christ, it becomes a priority to make Him the focal point of your life and seek to please Him above all else.

As we humbly position ourselves before the Lord, we open the door for His transformative work to take place within us. We don't have to know it all. Just for a moment, try to picture yourself looking in the mirror and seeing yourself as God does.

Indeed, it is truly remarkable that despite having complete knowledge about every aspect of our lives, God continues to shower us with His unwavering love. Nothing is a surprise to Him. Step into His presence, bring those issues that have been weighing you down, and He will help lift the burdens off of your shoulders. In order to find peace, it is important to start by forgiving yourself. Once you have done that, you can follow in the footsteps of Jesus and extend forgiveness to those who have wronged you. Forgiveness is a choice.

Total surrender is a transformative process that requires us to let go of control and loosen our grip on the things we have held onto tightly. It is about wholeheartedly embracing Jesus and following Him.

> *Jesus said to all of his followers, "If you truly desire to be my disciple, you must disown your life completely, embrace my 'cross' as your own, and surrender to my ways."*
>
> —Luke 9:23 (TPT)

Following Jesus is not merely a duty, but rather a choice that comes from the depths of one's heart. It is both a privilege and an honor. Indeed, it is a common experience for individuals to navigate through life with a set of dreams and goals they hope to accomplish. Like many individuals, I, too, received the same guidance of excelling in academics, pursuing higher education, and selecting a profession that would provide financial stability for self-sufficiency. Throughout our lives, we often find ourselves consumed with our own needs and desires, overlooking the One who selflessly sacrificed His life for our sake.

I went to college with the goal of becoming a court reporter. After graduating I entered the field and started my professional journey. However, throughout my career,

I found myself constantly struggling with a sense of dissatisfaction with my work. I thought, This can't be it. Still unsure of what I wanted to do for work, I found myself returning to college multiple times in an attempt to explore different degree options. No matter what I did, I never felt satisfied. You might be wondering, Why? The reason for this is that I attempted to fulfill a role that was not aligned with my true calling.

Many times, we find ourselves searching for answers that are right in front of us. The Bible says:

> *Make God the utmost delight and pleasure of your life, and he will provide for you what you desire the most.*
> —Psalm 37:4 (TPT)

How many times have you prayed for something, just to find out that God had answered your prayer? I was asking for more of Him, and it seemed like I was getting what I asked for. I yearned to be in His presence. I dare you to make Jesus the focal point of your life, and then watch what happens as a direct result of your decision to do so. As He becomes more significant, everything else fades into the background. Your goals and outlook on life will shift as a result of this. You will start to see things in a completely different light.

Prayer:

Heavenly Father, forgive me for being so self-centered. I give up the ability to direct my own life. My only goal is to please You. Carry out a work in me from the inside out so that I can be set free and fulfill the purpose for which You have designed me. In Jesus's name. Amen.

PART III

Freedom in Christ

CHAPTER 5
The Truth Will Set You Free

> *For if you embrace the truth, it will release more freedom into your lives.*
> —John 8:32 (TPT)

Your life will change when you start seeing yourself the way God sees you. Each one of us plays a role in God's master plan. It is up to us to figure out what our purpose is and to get in line with what He wants. Individuals who lack a clear vision and wander aimlessly are unlikely to make any meaningful progress. On the other hand, those who possess the ability to envision their desired life are more likely to make significant strides towards their goals. The outcome of your journey will be influenced by your perspective and the direction in which you envision yourself progressing.

> *Where there is no vision, the people perish: but he that keepeth the law, happy is he.*
>
> —Proverbs 29:18 (AV)

Understand that the devil enjoys twisting things to serve his purposes. For many years, whenever I glanced in the mirror, I was confronted with an image that was difficult for me to look at. I strongly suggest that you invest in a mirror and make it a daily habit to examine your reflection. It's important to recognize and embrace your own unique beauty. Remind yourself daily that you have a special place in this world and that your life holds meaning. Trust that there is a path laid out specifically for you. Never forget the extent of God's love for you. Remind yourself that if you have accepted the gift of salvation, you have become a new creation in Christ. When you look in the mirror at some point in the future, you will see an entirely different person. You will be able to see yourself as God does, and He will reveal to you what your mission in life is. Nobody else can carry out the task that God has ordained specifically for you to do.

The reality is that God is not impressed with how many degrees a person has, what they look like, or how many followers and likes they have on social media. As we shift our focus from society's perception of value to God's perception of value, we will begin to experience greater levels of freedom.

Since I was a young child, my breasts have always been on the smaller side. At the age of eighteen, I made the decision to proceed with breast augmentation surgery. Since I was still unhappy with the size and wanted to achieve a certain look, I underwent the procedure multiple times. You most likely have questions regarding the purpose of this ongoing behavior. Everything boils down to the thoughts that we choose to entertain. Magazines, reality programs, and social media are all contributing to the spread of misleading information, which is especially harmful to young people who are still developing their identity. Because of this, we have to look to the Word of God to discover who we are.

There are instances where elective surgery may be a reasonable choice. The motive behind it is what truly matters. Are your efforts done in vain? As a temple of the Holy Spirit, we must treat our bodies with respect. We should not be so concerned with how we look. I attempted to fill the void within me by chasing after acceptance and the praise of others. Individuals often tend to judge others based on their outward appearance, whereas God focuses on the true nature of a person by looking at their heart.

> *But the Lord said to Samuel, "Do not look at his appearance or at the height of his stature, because I have rejected him.*

> *For the Lord sees not as man sees; for man looks at the outward appearance, but the Lord looks at the heart."*
> —1 Samuel 16:7 (AMP)

To become a court reporter, I took on a mountain of student loan debt and piled on countless hours of training. Nothing about the experience nourished my soul. None of your successes, regardless of how impressive they may be, can assist you in fulfilling your purpose in life. You will never feel content with your life if you do not pursue the path that your heart guides you toward. Jesus is the ultimate source of freedom and fulfillment. Embrace a life of limitless possibilities in Him.

When children do not experience love or support within their family, they often find themselves searching for those essential elements in other places. Indeed, the influence of a father is truly profound. The absence of love from my father drove me to seek it elsewhere. The desire to feel loved is something that resonates with everyone. In Deuteronomy 31:6, we find a beautiful promise that assures us of unending love and friendship. It states, "He will never leave you nor forsake you." Rest assured, you are never alone.

The condition of our hearts is what is important to God. It is something that can only be seen by Him and no one else. When you submit your life to the authority of Jesus Christ, you are given a new identity. Jesus serves as the ultimate source of your true identity. He reveals who you truly are at the very essence of your being.

> *So above all, guard the affections of your heart, for they affect all that you are. Pay attention to the welfare of your innermost being, for from there flows the wellspring of life.*
> —Proverbs 4:23 (TPT)

We are cautioned to guard our hearts because what happens there can damage every aspect of who we are. My heart has been pierced. It has been injured, and it has been left broken, just like the hearts of some of you who are reading this. Some of it was due to my own actions, and some of it was due to the actions of others. Before I dealt with my heart, which is, by the way, an ongoing process, it was difficult for me to love myself and accept what God's word said about me. We can't just pretend that our wounds do not exist and act like nothing happened. When you try to cover weeds with dirt, what kind of results do you get? They gradually come back into view.

I was able to let go of the pain and exchange it with God's love as I dealt with the issues that were weighing on my heart, spent time with Him, and repented. Even the most severe wounds can be healed by His love.

I understand that some of you may have doubts about how God could still love you considering everything you've been through. I used to have the same perspective. The good news is that whenever we turn from our sins and seek God's forgiveness, He does so right away. He cleanses us of those sins.

> *And now you must repent and turn back to God so that your sins will be removed, and so that times of refreshing will stream from the Lord's presence.*
> —Acts 3:19 (TPT)

You have a choice: you can allow the pain and trauma to remain buried and allow it to continue to afflict you, or you can make the decision to repent, forgive yourself and those who have wronged you, and be set free from the chains of the past. We need to put our pride aside and address the problems that we face. You won't be able to see the need for change if you don't first acknowledge there is a problem, but ultimately, the choice is yours to make. Because of repentance, I was able to turn away from my sins and continue on with my life, secure in the knowledge that God would forgive me no matter what I did. Once I had reconciled with

God, I was able to approach Him without feeling ashamed. As we spend more time with Jesus, we grow in our likeness to Him.

> *We can all draw close to him with the veil removed from our faces. And with no veil we all become like mirrors who brightly reflect the glory of the Lord Jesus. We are being transfigured into his very image as we move from one brighter level of glory to another. And this glorious transfiguration comes from the Lord, who is the Spirit.*
> —2 Corinthians 3:18 (TPT)

When you know who you are in Christ, the opinions and actions of others will hold no power over you. It has no effect on you anymore. The approval of God is the only approval that truly matters.

The truth is this: you are loved. You are here for a reason. For you, God sacrificed His only Son. According to 1 Corinthians 6:19–20, you were bought with a price. You were actually purchased with the precious blood of Jesus and made His own. You no longer need to feel guilty about any of the sins you committed in the past, since they are all forgiven in full. No matter the trial you may be currently facing or the uncertain path that lies ahead, God's love for you will never change. Nothing can ever separate you from the love of God (Romans 8:38–39).

When I finally gained an understanding of what the Bible says about me, I had no choice but to change the words I was speaking. For the better part of my life, I have maintained a critical attitude toward not only myself but also the circumstances in which I have found myself. Words are far more potent than I had originally thought. Words have the power to bless or to curse in equal measure. Your own words have the power to either construct or destroy your future, depending on how you choose to use them. I began speaking words of life and purpose over myself and forced myself to do things, even when I didn't feel like it.

Throughout the day, I would remind myself that I am a child of God (John 1:12), chosen (Ephesians 1:4), and capable of accomplishing all things through His strength and empowerment (Philippians 4:13). I began taking my son on walks in the neighborhood on a regular basis. He delighted in spending time outside, and we both benefited immensely from the warmth of the sun and fresh air. The worst action you can take is no action at all. At first, it was challenging since I had to train myself on how to *tame my tongue*, as the saying goes.

Death and life are in the power of our tongue (Proverbs 18:21). It is important that we watch what we say and do not let the words of others shape who we are or how we live our lives. Let us bless one another with the words that come out of our mouths and model such behavior for our children to follow.

> *Your words are so powerful that they will kill or give life, and the talkative person will reap the consequences.*
> —Proverbs 18:21 (TPT)

Prayer:

Heavenly Father, thank You for Your word, which teaches me about who I am in Christ. Help me to follow in Your footsteps, adopt a positive mindset, and carefully choose my words so I only speak words of life over myself, my loved ones, and anybody else I come in contact with. I rebuke and renounce anything unfavorable that has been spoken over me and my family, and I receive everything that You have for me. In the name of Jesus. Amen.

CHAPTER 6
Renewing the Mind for a New Beginning

> *And do not be conformed to this world [any longer with its superficial values and customs], but be transformed and progressively changed [as you mature spiritually] by the renewing of your mind [focusing on godly values and ethical attitudes], so that you may prove [for yourselves] what the will of God is, that which is good and acceptable and perfect [in His plan and purpose for you].*
> —Romans 12:2 (AMP)

Indeed, the power of the human mind is truly remarkable. It is the place where numerous decisions are made, and it has the potential to be filled with either faith or fear. If allowed to remain, fear has the potential to cripple an individual. Fear is not from God, but rather an emotion that can often cloud our judgment and hinder our ability to trust in God's plan for us.

> *For God did not give us a spirit of timidity or cowardice or fear, but [He has given us a spirit] of power and of love and of sound judgment and personal discipline [abilities that result in a calm, well-balanced mind and self-control].*
> —2 Timothy 1:7 (AMP)

I used to live in so much fear. There are numerous things that I used to sit and dwell on. I used to worry and come up with all the *what-ifs* in my mind. In the past, my mind would sometimes wander, taking me down paths that were less than pleasant. A continual battle raged within my mind. There were times when I was completely unable to escape my own thoughts. It seemed as if they were following my every move. I learned that in order to triumph over destructive thoughts, I needed to "take every thought captive," as it says in 2 Corinthians 10:5, and war against every thought by using the Word of God as my weapon. I would jot verses from the Bible down on note cards and have them with me at all times. I would force myself to stand up if I was sitting to get off of what I was thinking about, and then I would say out loud, "No, I take every thought captive and make it obedient to Christ." After that, I would verbally recite the scripture that was written on the note card. I had to immediately put an end to the falsehood, get rid of it, and then replace it with the truth.

> *Casting down imaginations, and every high thing that exalteth itself against the knowledge of God, and bringing into captivity every thought to the obedience of Christ…*
> —2 Corinthians 10:5 (AV)

Where do you plan to direct the majority of your focus? A person has the option of spending their time sitting around and watching the news, which may cause them to feel anxious, or they may choose to read the Bible and spend time with Jesus, which may assist them in strengthening their faith. Whatever it is that you focus your attention on expands to fill the space that it occupies in your mind. If you make the decision to focus on the difficulties you are facing, those challenges will become even more insurmountable, making them even more difficult for you to overcome. When you focus your attention on God, He will occupy the space in your heart and mind that you have prepared for Him. The Bible advises us to center our thoughts on heavenly things.

> *Set your mind and keep focused habitually on the things above [the heavenly things], not on things that are on the earth [which have only temporal value].*
> —Colossians 3:2 (AMP)

Prevent your thoughts from meandering aimlessly. Make a conscious effort to concentrate on heavenly matters. You have two options: you can choose to stay where you are and keep being tormented, or you can make the decision to improve your condition by surrendering to God and standing up against the adversary. The Bible is the most powerful weapon that God has given us.

> *So then, surrender to God. Stand up to the devil and resist him and he will turn and run away from you.*
> —James 4:7 (TPT)

When I finally decided to put up a fight, things started to turn around for me. I would lie in bed for hours wallowing in self-pity and having what you might call a pity party, but this would just make the problem even more difficult to deal with. I was aware that I could not carry on acting in the same manner that I had been. It was necessary for me to adjust the way that I thought, spoke, and acted. Because I had never done that before, it required a lot of work on my part to finally get around to doing it. I needed a new beginning so badly at that point. I had no choice except to separate myself from the outside world and seek God.

Make it a habit to spend time with Jesus every day. Find a nice, quiet place where you can unwind and put your worries behind you. First, rest in a comfortable position, close your eyes, and take a few long, deep breaths. Then draw a deeper breath in, and once you've done that, let go of all of your worries and the stress that's been building up in your body. Relax; there is nothing to worry about. Focus all of your affection on Jesus. He is worthy of it all. Continue to wait on Jesus while taking a few slow, deep breaths and focusing on your breathing. As soon as you become aware of His presence, grant Him permission to minister to you and be open to receiving what He is doing within you.

Have patience with yourself and remain open to being shaped and molded by Him throughout the process. This will take some time. Before you know it, you'll start looking forward to the time you get to spend with Him.

It's true that change might be uncomfortable, but remember that it's for the best. After I started on this path, I found that I could approach both people and problems in a different way. It took some work, but I was finally able to let go of my resentment and forgive my father. I led him to a saving faith in Christ right before he passed away. My dad's life was cut short. As a consequence of this, he was unable to accomplish all of the plans that God had set forth for his life. We must each work out our own salvation. My father's life was taken from him much too soon, just like my mother's was. Despite being saved, my father did not experience true freedom during his time on earth. Since he has gone to be with the Lord, he is at peace.

I pray that you will find the strength to forgive, so that Jesus might bring about the much-needed inner healing. There you can finally break free. You are not defined by your past. Women play a crucial role in bringing the next generation into the world. When we embrace God's healing, we can experience true freedom. This freedom empowers us to effectively guide our children in the ways of the Lord and to lay a solid foundation, not only for ourselves but also for the generations that will come after us.

I was able to put a stop to the lies and negative voices that had been troubling my mind with the assistance of the Holy Spirit, who led me to find the truth about who I am in Christ. I could see that light was beginning to emerge, and the darkness was beginning to fade. By illuminating the source of my distress, the Holy Spirit enabled me to conquer my fears, anxieties, and worries. I have accepted and even come to embrace the person I am, and I now see myself as a victor. Even in the present day, I may face challenges, but I refuse to let them determine the path my life will take.

In an effort to cure postpartum depression, I did seek treatment from a psychologist as well as a psychiatrist, and I was also prescribed a number of different medications to help alleviate the symptoms. But in the end, it was my faith in Jesus Christ that allowed me to get to the place that I am at now. I am of the opinion that each and every person was created for a specific reason, and I believe that when we are able to look beyond our present situation, we will be able to rise above it and fulfill our destiny.

It took me a year to fully recover from postpartum depression. The desperation drove me to a point where I had no choice but to confront the deep and secret issues that had been tormenting me throughout my life. I do not ever want to go through something like that again. Surprisingly, this extremely difficult journey ultimately transformed me in a positive way.

In order to give the support that a mother and her family might require when suffering with postpartum depression, it may be necessary to draw from a wide variety of resources. It's okay if you don't find your path to healing at the office of a therapist, psychologist, or psychiatrist.

Finding the missing piece of the puzzle is ultimately what it comes down to. I believe that we are all on a journey, and our job is to love others regardless of where they are on their path and to assist them in the healing process, which looks different for each person depending on their history and their current circumstances. You can be of assistance to a sick individual by recommending that they get treatment from a medical professional. If an individual wishes to seek healing via alternative means, I believe it is just as important to refer them to a Christian counselor or prayer minister. It is not necessary for the knowledge that we gather from books to serve as the driving force behind our own personal healing process.

The bond that exists between a mother and her child is a precious one. It is my belief that it is important for mothers to feel loved in order for them to be able to express this love to their children and direct them towards a path illuminated by the divine presence of Jesus. The enemy is aware that if he is successful in attacking the mother, he would be able to cause havoc for the entire family. This is due to the fact that women typically spend the most time caring for their children.

Everyone desires to have their voice heard. Know that you are not alone, and you are not the only one who has ever felt the way you do right now. The first step toward healing is admitting there is a problem. I believe that showing someone who is going through tough times that you care about them and are there for them is one of the best gifts you could offer them, and it doesn't cost anything. After coming to terms with the magnitude of God's love for me, I was able to see that my life has both a purpose and a path that must be pursued.

Whenever I have the opportunity to speak to a woman who is suffering in silence, I make it a priority to understand where she is in her journey, offer her the necessary resources for her and her family, and provide encouragement for whatever challenges she may be facing.

You are beautiful.
You are valued.
You are loved.
No one can replace you.

These words may appear simple at first glance, but they hold profound meaning. They possess the power to significantly impact someone's life, especially a new mother who is navigating through challenging times.

There will always be obstacles in our path, but if we can find a way to support one another through them, the end result will be different. I am able to give testimony to this. At the time of my father's passing, I was three months along in the pregnancy with my second child. Moving forward in time to November of that same year, I went into labor six weeks before my due date. The Word of God was substituted for every unfavorable report that was given by the physicians, and as a result, my son was delivered in excellent health.

My second pregnancy and delivery were substantially different from the first time around. With the love and support of my loved ones and the reassurance of God's promises, I knew that things would work out for the best. These things combined gave me the confidence that I needed.

If someone assures you that there are no problems, but you have a sense that there could be one, question them for additional information and try to get to the bottom of things by learning as much as you can about the situation. If we work together and collaborate, we will be able to accomplish more.

Everyone who is currently reading this book possesses something that has the potential to assist another person in overcoming an obstacle and catapulting them into the destiny that God has intended for them. God will often provide support to those in need through the lives of other people. This nurse that my husband and I met in the emergency room was kind enough to provide us her contact information, and as a result, I was able to meet with her. We became friends, and she made the introduction that led to me being given the opportunity to speak about my experience at a postpartum support conference. The glory belongs to God. Because of all the people God has brought into my life to assist me in overcoming postpartum depression, I will be eternally thankful to Him. When we work together, we become stronger as the body of Christ. There is power in unity.

You will discover that as you put Jesus at the center of your life and nurture your relationship with the Holy Spirit, He directs you toward the kind of life you have only dreamed of having. Even when things appear to be at their worst, He will never leave your side and will instead serve as a compass for you. If you are going through a difficult time in your life, you can have peace of mind knowing that, if you commit your way to God and put your faith in Him, He will help you triumph over it.

> *Trust God from the bottom of your heart; don't try to figure out everything on your own.*
> *Listen for God's voice in everything you do, everywhere you go; he's the one who will keep you on track.*
> *Don't assume that you know it all. Run to God! Run from evil!*
> *Your body will glow with health, your very bones will vibrate with life!*
> —Proverbs 3:5–8 (MSG)

Every day is a gift from God. Did you know that the moment you get up, you can take authority over and command your day? You can choose not to be affected by the activities going on around you. "This is the day the Lord has made and I will rejoice and be glad in it" (Psalm 118:24). Determine that today will be a good day for you because "today is the day that the Lord has made." You are able to make the decision that you will stand against the devil because "greater is he that is in you, than he that is in the world" (1 John 4:4). If "you and your household are going to serve the Lord" (Joshua 24:15), then you must determine that you are going to be the mother that God has called you to be. Even when it seems like there is no way out of any situation, don't ever let go!

Instead,

> *Arise [from spiritual depression to a new life], shine [be radiant with the glory and brilliance of the Lord]; for your light has come, and the glory and brilliance of the Lord has risen upon you.*
> —Isaiah 60:1 (AMP)

Persevere through the darkness, for it is in these times of testing that we discover the true strength within ourselves. Please take some time to read the following chapter and allow its life-giving words to reverberate within the depths of your heart.

> *The Spirit of the Lord God is upon me,*
> *Because the Lord has anointed and*
> *commissioned me*

*To bring good news to the humble and afflicted;
He has sent me to bind up [the wounds of] the brokenhearted,
To proclaim release [from confinement and condemnation] to the [physical and spiritual] captives
And freedom to prisoners,
To proclaim the favorable year of the Lord,
And the day of vengeance and retribution of our God,
To comfort all who mourn,
To grant to those who mourn in Zion the following:
To give them a turban instead of dust [on their heads, a sign of mourning],
The oil of joy instead of mourning,
The garment [expressive] of praise instead of a disheartened spirit.
So they will be called the trees of righteousness [strong and magnificent, distinguished for integrity, justice, and right standing with God],
The planting of the Lord, that He may be glorified.
Then they will rebuild the ancient ruins,*

They will raise up and restore the former desolations;
And they will renew the ruined cities,
The desolations (deserted settlements) of many generations.
Strangers will stand and feed your flocks,
And foreigners will be your farmers and your vinedressers.
But you shall be called the priests of the Lord;
People will speak of you as the ministers of our God.
You will eat the wealth of nations,
And you will boast of their riches.
Instead of your [former] shame you will have a double portion;
And instead of humiliation your people will shout for joy over their portion.
Therefore in their land they will possess double [what they had forfeited];
Everlasting joy will be theirs.
For I, the Lord, love justice;
I hate robbery with a burnt offering.
And I will faithfully reward them,
And make an everlasting covenant with them.

*Then their offspring will be known
among the nations,
And their descendants among the peoples.
All who see them [in their prosperity]
will recognize and acknowledge them
That they are the people whom the Lord
has blessed.
I will rejoice greatly in the Lord,
My soul will exult in my God;
For He has clothed me with garments of
salvation,
He has covered me with a robe of
righteousness,
As a bridegroom puts on a turban,
And as a bride adorns herself with her
jewels.
For as the earth brings forth its sprouts,
And as a garden causes what is sown in it
to spring up,
So the Lord God will [most certainly]
cause righteousness and justice and praise
To spring up before all the nations
[through the power of His word].*
—Isaiah 61 (AMP)

That is intended for you, my friend! You will not suffer this affliction any longer. He is calling you higher into a new life in Him, and He is calling you out to the world. Answer the call, and let your light shine brightly, illuminating the path for others to follow.

The trials of postpartum depression have truly been a humbling experience. Indeed, the impact of it has completely transformed my life. My identity is deeply rooted in Christ, and I have found peace and fulfillment in being a stay-at-home mom. I am grateful for Daniel, my amazing husband. Together we have made the decision to homeschool our incredible boys, who are currently seven and nine years old. They hold a special place in my heart. Realizing how quickly my sons are growing up, I try to soak up as much time as I can with them. As a tight-knit family, we do everything together. The boys have a lot of fun at playgrounds and parks, where they may run about and play unrestricted.

Throughout the journey, I've realized how vital it is to count my blessings and live in the here and now. I found myself in a place I never could have foreseen, yet somehow, it feels right. Motherhood is a genuinely incredible adventure that requires a great deal of selflessness, unflinching patience, and the ability to put one's own needs and desires to the side. To avoid becoming overwhelmed by the seemingly endless list of chores that need to be done around the house, I try to keep my attention on the tasks at hand. I tell myself that I'll get to these things eventually and that tomorrow is always an option.

Indeed, the journey of motherhood possesses a remarkable ability to unlock doors, revealing a deeper understanding of God's love. These doors, which might have otherwise remained closed, are opened wide by the transformative power of nurturing and raising children. I will always be on a journey of learning and growth, flexibly adjusting to the winds of change. This ongoing process has played a significant role in shaping me into a stronger and more compassionate person, not only in my roles as a wife and mother but in all aspects of my life. I have discovered a love that I had long been seeking. It is through my connection with Christ that this love has been awakened within me, and now I am blessed with the ability to extend it to my beloved family and those around me.

As you contemplate the decision of whether to remain at home or return to work, it's important to keep in mind the incredible potential that lies within you and your family. You are destined for greatness, and there is truly no greater joy than nurturing children who hold a deep love for the Lord. My hope is that your story intertwines with His, and that as you navigate through motherhood, you also discover your true identity in Christ. Take heart, for the blessings that Jesus has graciously bestowed upon me are also within your reach.

Prayer:

Heavenly Father, thank You for the gift of your Son, Jesus. As I spend time in Your presence, unveil the depths and radiant brilliance that reside within You. I am grateful for a new beginning and for drawing me into Your light. I pray that everything I do is geared toward one thing: bringing honor to You. In Jesus's name. Amen.

If you are enduring difficulties and could benefit from some prayer, please contact me at shirleymotorca@gmail.com.

I'd be delighted to hear from you. I am neither a doctor or a mental health professional, but I do know the Great Physician.

www.ingramcontent.com/pod-product-compliance
Lightning Source LLC
LaVergne TN
LVHW010556070526
838199LV00063BA/4991